AF571957

The Best Cartoons from
Leadership
Journal
Volume 6

The Best Cartoons from Leadership Journal

Volume 6

Nashville, Tennessee

Published by Broadman & Holman Publishers,
Nashville, Tennessee
Editorial Team: Leonard G. Goss, John Landers

0-8054-2157-2

Dewey Decimal Classification: 817
Subject Heading: HUMOR

01 02 03 04 05 04 03 02 01 00

COMPLAINTS
PORTLOCK

PLEASE NO DOZING!
THANK YOU FOR NOT COUGHING
KEEP BABIES QUIET
ABSOLUTELY NO DIGRESSIONS!
PLEASE FINISH BY NOON.
DON'T FORGET ILLUSTRATIONS!
SUGGS

“Of course, feel free anytime to let me know what you think of the job I’m doing as your pastor.”

“What else about my sermon didn’t you like?”

STOP
STOP
STOP
STOP
STOP
STOP
STOP
STOP
STOP
STOP
STOP
PORTLOCK

"And here is Mr. Elmer W. Durham with a dissenting view from last week's sermon."

Pastor Wayne Klemper didn't respond well to criticism.

Church Discipline

SHOOT.
I DID IT AGAIN. I STRONGLY DISAGREED, YET SAID, "GOOD SERMON, PASTOR."
Dan Pegoda

“My dad says a two-hour sermon
is an impeachable offense.”

REPORT
ATTEND-104
OFFER-1,853
FEELINGS HURT-26
ANGRY- 12
IT'S BEEN A BETTER WEEK THAN USUAL
TAPP

LIKED SERMON ↓
DIDN'T LIKE SERMON USE BASEMENT EXIT
PORTLOCK

After-Church Coffee with Siskel and Ebert
ROGER, we got his whole point in the FIRST FIVE MINUTES!
Dan Pegoda

AGREE
DISAGREE
JOSEPH FARRIS

PORTLOCK

Pastor Marv knew it wasn't his best sermon ever, but he wasn't prepared for this.

"Of course, when I said, 'In conclusion,' I never expected a response like this!"

BRILLIANT!: Ø
GREAT SERMON: II
GOOD SERMON: HHT HHT HHT HHT III
HEY, THANKS: HHT II
SO, HOW'S IT GOIN'?: III
Hey, thanks.
Dan Pegoda

"Pastor, your new office furniture is ready."

COMPLAINTS
mouton-Chambers

Despite his increasing frustration, Pastor Grant was not going to publicly reverse his open-door policy.

"Yes, my door is always open—now get out of here!"

THANK YOU
FOR NOT SMOKING
THANK YOU
FOR NOT STAYING
TOO LONG
THANK YOU FOR
NOT BRINGING
UP INERRANCY
PASTOR TODD

"With our current hard feelings, would anyone object to my praying with my eyes open?"

Reverend Steen's Position on a Few of the Tougher Issues

“It’s time to be prophetic,” you said.
“No more mincing words . . .”

"I'm here to report the decisions from our recent board meeting . . . and I'll be brief."

"I thought it might be an appropriate time to give a sermon on anger."

"They're always eager to get into the woods during deer season. Just don't say anything controversial."

"Welcome to the church. Would you care to join a coup against the current pastor?"

"What makes you think there's a revolution afoot, Pastor?"

“What makes you think I’ve got problems with my staff?”

"I think I *need* to refer you to a church that *specializes* in forgiveness."

"It was a church split. But they decided to remain friends for the sake of their children."

"That was our contemporary service. Next is the traditional service, followed by a classical service, and a casual service with a sports emphasis."

"I suppose that solves the problem of which side the piano goes on."

PORTLOCK

"This flock is okay, but I prefer feeding in pastures a different shade of green."

"Before we begin our special congregational meeting, let's all stand and sing 'Blest Be the Tie that Binds.' "

"Remember the 'anxious bench'?
We call it the 'angry bench.' "

"It's come to my attention that there's been a minor split in the church."

Foi 'ər
Foi 'ā
JOHNSON

Quick, Jenkins! Theyre dividing again!
Dan Pegoda

Sunday morning's guest speaker miraculously averts a church split.

"Bernice, do you think when we sing the worship choruses you could play a bit more casually?"

"They donated it, but they didn't care for the offertory today."

"Boy, it's great to get away from the church for an afternoon and not have to think about all the conflict."

"First, let me ask, Rev. Farlow:
Are you under a lot of stress?"

"Looks like Pastor White's going through another trial."

© 1989 Erik Johnson

"Actually, this is my son, the pastor.
He never learned to handle stress very well."

"It's called the Be-All-Things-to-All-People Exercise Program."

"I told you Pastor Roberts hates Monday appointments."

Now I'll be happy!

"And while I've got you up here, Pastor, let me tell you what's wrong with the church."

JOHNSON
PASTOR'S
OFFICE
THE PASTOR IS:
JOLLY
AFFABLE
PREOCCUPIED
POUTING
FRANTIC
DANGEROUS

"The Pastor is in a good mood, and I'm NOT going to let you ruin it."

"Pastor, I'm having a little problem with a friend. I'm wondering if you'd have a chat with him."

"You were right. Talking through the problem brought us to an agreement—that it's all your fault."

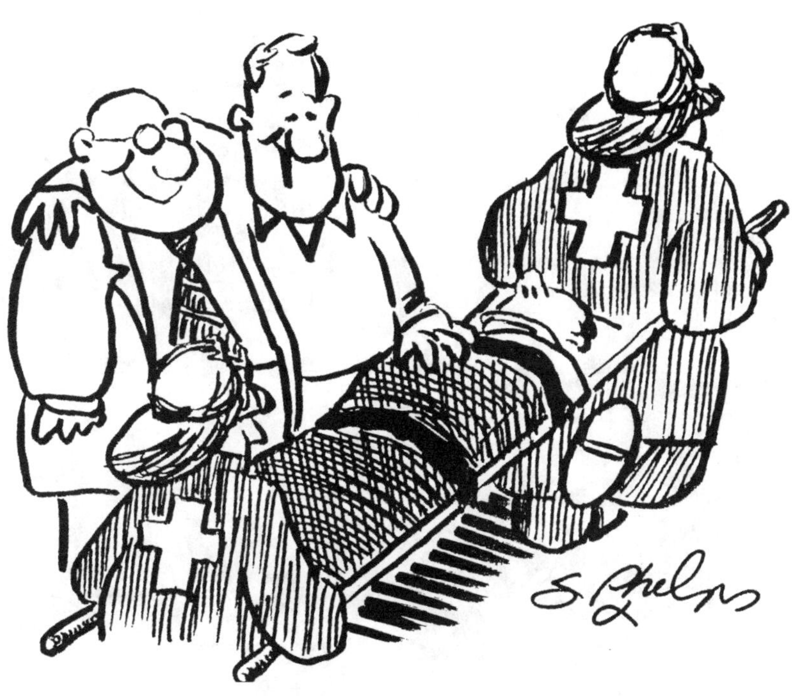

"Pastor, we appreciate you helping us resolve our petty disagreement."

"Thanks for the marriage counseling, Pastor.
We feel much better."

"I hate his approach to counseling!"

"At nine, you meet with skepticism, at ten you meet with resistance, at noon, you meeet with ridicule and derision."

"This isn't a holdup, Pastor. I just want your undivided attention for a minute."

"I came to you because I can't go back to my last three pastors . . . are you familiar with restraining orders?"

"When he says 'gimmie that old time religion,' he means he wants a crusty old guy, just like him, to be his pastor."

"I take it there's something you haven't told me."

"Of course this is confidential. Why did you ask?"

"Impersonal in what way, Jones, Mr. Henry M.?"

"The athletes in the congregation say I should be more athletic. The businessmen say I should be more businesslike. Fred, I admit, I'm worried about what YOU'RE going to say."

"Pastor, do you honestly think adding a full-time counselor to our staff will help our church to grow? I, for one, do not see any way it can. All we'll do is attract a bunch of complaining, negative-thinking whiners who can't see the possibilities in anything. Boy, I hate complainers, don't you, Pastor? They're just a bunch of time wasters. I vote no with a capital N because the last thing we need around here is a bunch of negative-thinking, do-nothing complainers . . ."

"I've never been good at repentance, Pastor. I'll just let you use my condo during August, and God can call it even."

"I'm afraid this is a bit out of my league, Mrs. Bosley."

"Pastor Smith wouldn't hold a grudge over a little thing like that . . . would he?"

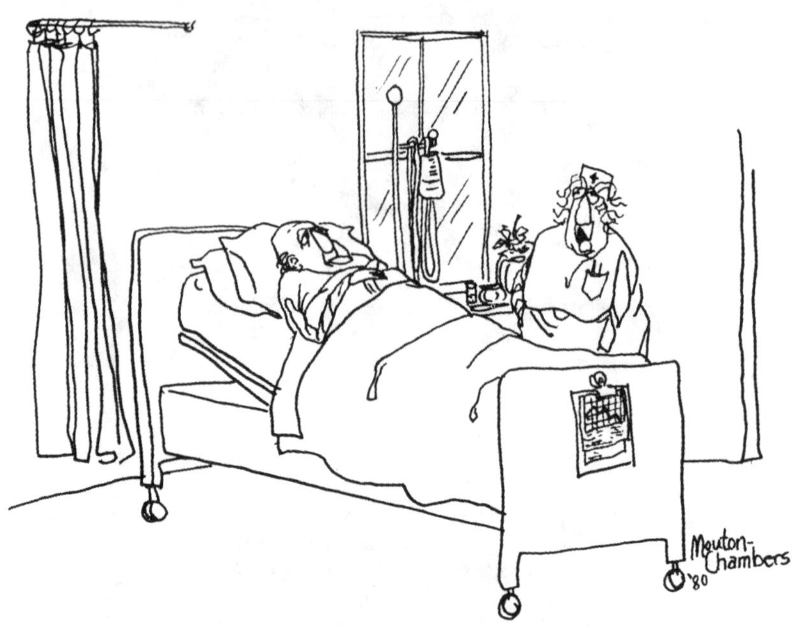

"Good news, Reverend. The board has voted to pray for your recovery . . . the vote was 5-4."

Pastor Bob didn't think the board received his threatened resignation in the proper spirit.

"Well, gentlemen, Robert's Rules doesn't seem to specify whether prayer should come *before* or *after* the call to order."

Pastor Marvin prepares for his meeting with the chairman of the board.

"I'd like to thank the board for this lovely plant after our disagreement this week."

Pastor White and the Seven Deacons: Sneezy, Doc, Bashful, Grumpy, Happy, Sleepy, and Absentee.

"Of course I know what an agitator is. I've worked with deacons for 10 years, haven't I?"

"And Lord, we thank you that we stand united
after this unanimous board decision."

"I don't have time for this, Stan!
We'll talk about it at the business meeting."

"Things seem a little unsettled here after last night's board meeting, Dear."

"Miss Simmons? The program people are at my east door, and the building people are at my west door. I'm going to lunch."

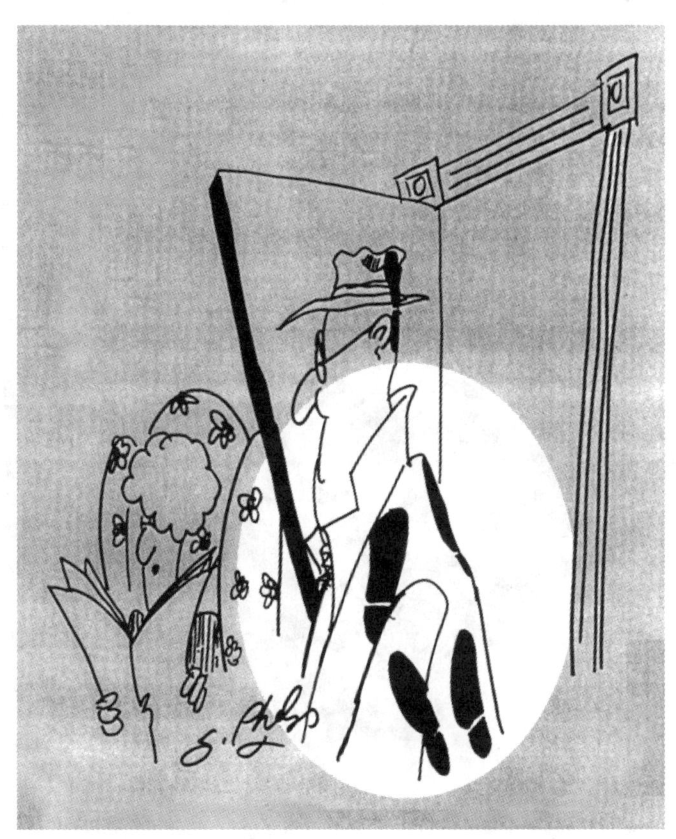

"So, how was your board meeting?"

"But look on the bright side. You did win the vote."

Reverend Sheldon patiently waits for the board chairman to call and apologize.

"Pastor! Henderson here is not agreeing to disagree!"

"Bad news, Bishop. Our church-planting team is divided on whether to call the new congregation 'First United Church' or 'United First Church.' "

"Pastor, we've been hired by the kitchen committee to determine who last used the church kitchen. May we have a few words with you?"

"Most of us are committed to furthering God's kingdom. We're not quite sure what Hawkins is committed to furthering."

"In the minutes, should I record this as a 'vigorous theological discussion' or a 'serious ecclesiastical debate'?"

"So last night we of the decorating committee were able to hammer out our differences and agree on a plan."

In the quietness of his office, Pastor Maurice contemplates the resignation of the chairman of the board of trustees.

Pastor Gridley discovers a rather effective means of filing board member complaints.

Pastor Bob dealt with a disagreeable board member in his own unique way.

Pastor Randall walks to his car after a tough board meeting and . . . deja vu!

"We have a preacher who wants to lead the music, a song leader who wants to preach, an organist who wants to head up the elder board. Now all we need is an elder who wants to play the organ."

"Okay, this is better. Now about the little disagreement we had back in the board room . . ."

"Just because the board chairman wants to throw his weight around doesn't mean you have to."

"Now about the differences regarding Sunday school curriculum . . ."

"The Wednesday Bible Study, Saturday Prayer Breakfast, Crib Nursery, and Women's Mission Society have declared their independence and will exist as a commonwealth with details regarding defense to be worked out at a later date."

"How did the singles group respond to your suggestion that they call themselves 'The Leftovers'?"

"We interrupt this sermon to inform you that the 4th grade boys are now in complete control of their Sunday school class and are holding Miss Moseby hostage . . ."

“I want to thank you for the great job of leading the class. We usually can’t get anyone to discuss anything.”

"My last three visitors came in to lay down the law, lay a guilt trip on me, and lay it on the line. I wish I were a lay person!"

"Would you like a word with me, Mrs. Thundermuffin?"

"Pastor, I hate to complain, but I want to do what I do best."

"Hey, I wouldn't want to confront Mrs. Schultz either."

"Careful, Honey, she seems a little bitter."

116 DAYS
WITHOUT
A COMPLIMENT
Baloo

"Left town on my days off; how 'bout you?"

"It looks like Pastor must have had a hard week."

"Why can't he just read his resignation like other pastors do?"

"Our previous pastor resigned rather suddenly . . ."

"He got it into his head that he could lower his cholesterol more easily at another church."

The third day there, it hit Pastor Edmunds that the church had given him a *one*-*way* ticket.

“Dear Diary: Third week in new church.
Conflict aplenty. Sense challenges ahead . . .”

First Church
WEEK 3:
7 THINGS THIS
CHURCH NEEDS
TO CHANG
E
WELCOME
OUR
NEW PASTOR
Tim Liston

"The leather pews are nice, but what's a guy have to do to get a fresh cup of coffee around here?"

"Brother Thomas, here, will take your hat. Brother Feedlestein will take your coat, and Dr. Nicely will handle the baggage from your previous church."

"This will be your office. The boxes in the closet are for when you leave."

"Here we go. The return policy."

"His resignation announcement
is not as good as the last pastor's."

First Church
PASTOR BILL, WHEN YOU GET BACK FROM VACATION DON'T BOTHER COMING INTO THE OFFICE. JUST STOP BY THE TREASURER'S HOUSE FOR A MESSAGE AND TO PICK SOMETHING UP.
Tim Liston

A Bad Sign

You know it's time to leave when a preacher preaches on guilt, and he is the only one who feels guilty.

You know it's time to leave when the church changed the morning worship time, and they failed to notify you.

You know it's time to leave when the members of the pulpit committee that hired you are simultaneously missing from Sunday morning worship.

"Today's sermon is one I've wanted to preach for some time now . . ."

"Pastor, your ten o'clock counseling session and last Sunday's sermon illustration are here!"

"Unhand me, or I'll use you in a sermon illustration!"

"I'll give you a moment to reconsider that remark . . . before I put it in my next sermon."

"Just for your information, Pastor, Point Number One, Point Number Two, and all their little subpoints left in a huff during your closing story."

PASTOR KIDNEYFERN PLAYS THE GLAD GAME

"What I told you was confidential, and then what did you preach about on Sunday? Sin!"

"All persons in my sermon were fictitious . . . All persons in my sermon were fictitious . . . All persons . . ."

WORST MOMENTS *in Ministry*

Midway through his sermon illustration about "a couple from my last church," Pastor Filbert realizes they came for a surprise visit.

"Nothing personal . . . nothing personal . . .
nothing personal . . ."

"Don't you offer to shake my hand, Preacher, until you're ready to apologize for not having the sensitivity to know what I'm offended about!"

"And until next Sunday, remember . . . God loves you, I love you, and Brother Al here is working on it."

"You need to work on your attitude, Dave."

"Pastor, is it more blessed to be meek or to beat the devil out of 'em?"

"Today's sermon is on the most important theme of the Bible . . ."

"Got any OTHER books on conflict management?"

"Some of us have been discussing ways you could improve your preaching."

"Why can't he admit he's got a problem with staff turnover?"

Pastor's Nightmare #27:

"Where's my husband this morning? Right where you buried him last week."

"Look, Stan, I'm sorry about your car. But, frankly, I'm appalled that you, being a pastor, would allow yourself to become upset over something like this."

After a very brief discussion, the board of trustees dismissed Herb's charge that the church had become infatuated with youth.

"I think the first item on the agenda will be to unload our weapons."

"Officially, the results of the vote are forty 'yes,' seven 'no,' and one 'over my dead body.' "

"As we enter Advent, I'd like to remind the congregation that I can't stand fruitcake."

"That cloud looks like Mrs. Cheezeeder complaining about my hymn selections. That cloud over there looks like Mr. Barkwell complaining about the budget for youth ministry. That other cloud looks like Mrs. Lintcatcher complaining about the women's fellowship meetings . . ."

The SECRET of
PASTORAL
LONGEVITY:
FAILING THAT
NEW CHURCH JOB
INTERVIEW
johnson

"Next the children will recreate the church split that led to the founding of this church."